The Santero Ideal

The Art of Colorado Santera, Teresa May Duran

Second Edition

Netanel Miles-Yépez

Albion Andalus
Boulder, Colorado
2021

"The old shall be renewed,
and the new shall be made holy."
— Rabbi Avraham Yitzhak Kook

Albion-Andalus, Inc.
P. O. Box 19852
Boulder, CO 80308
www.albionandalus.com

Design and composition by Albion-Andalus, Inc.
Cover design by Albion-Andalus, Inc.
Cover image of the painting, "Christ" by Teresa May Duran.
Photos by Amitai Zachary Malone and Netanel Miles-Yépez.

Manufactured in the United States of America

ISBN: 978-1-953220-02-8 (HC)
ISBN: 978-1-7336589-1-1 (PB)

For

J.E.C.P.

Who shared my love of the New Mexico Territory
and its traditional arts

Table of Contents

Acknowledgments vii

Introduction 1

The Making of a Colorado Santera 3

The Art of a Colorado Santera 11

The Craft of a Colorado Santera 19

Afterword 25

Notes 27
Glossary 29
Biographies 30

Acknowledgments

I WISH TO thank Teresa May Duran for her kindness in discussing her life and work with me, as well as allowing me to publish this small monograph on that work. I must also thank Amitai Zachary Malone for taking some of the photographs used in this book, as well as Jennifer Elizabeth Phares, who accompanied me on the journey of exploring the work of many *santeros* across Colorado and New Mexico. Other friends who supported the book include Danice Crawford of Marisol Imports in Boulder, Colorado, as well as Tessa Bielecki and David Denny of Crestone, Colorado, who shared my interest in the Spanish Colonial arts of the American Southwest. Thank you to Erica Holland Leitz for reading the manuscript for errors.

— N.M-Y.

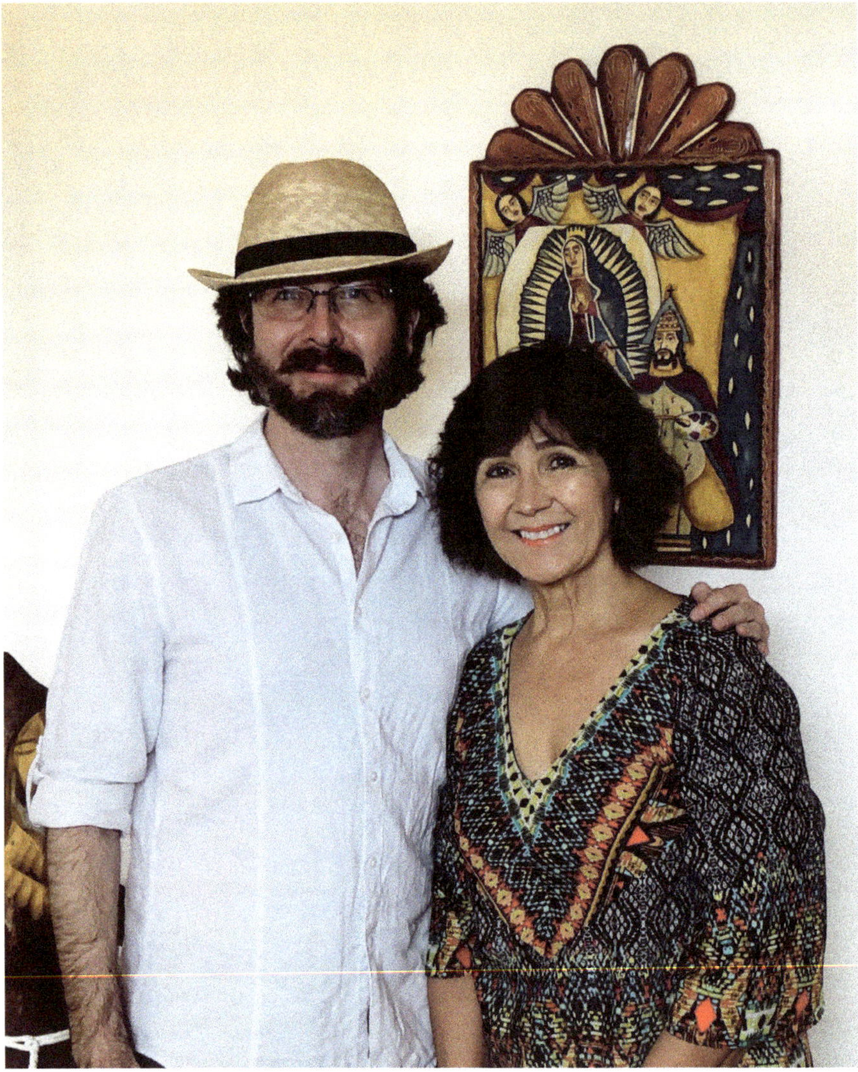

Netanel Miles-Yépez and Teresa May Duran posing with her original entry to the Spanish Market. (Photo by Ernest Duran, 2018)

Introduction

When one thinks of Spanish Colonial art in the Southwest it is usually of New Mexico and the famous Spanish Market of Santa Fe. But New Mexico isn't the only home of Spanish Colonial art and artists in the Southwest. Colorado also has an equally long tradition of these arts. In fact, the only reason we know less about them than those of New Mexico is because of a historical accident—*a change of borders*. Up until 1861, when the Colorado Territory was established, what is now southern Colorado up to the Arkansas River was actually the New Mexico Territory, and its arts and artists were one and the same. And yet, owing to this change of borders, the Spanish Colonial arts and artists of the modern state of Colorado have not received the same attention as those of New Mexico.

To remedy this situation, as both a Mexican-American artist and a scholar of religion, I set out in 2012 to document the lives and work of Colorado based *santeras* and *santeros*, the modern 'saint-makers' who have continued the traditional Spanish Colonial arts of the old New Mexico Territory. The intention was to choose four Colorado-based artists, documenting their lives and work, as well as their artistic and spiritual ideals in a book called, "The Santero Ideal." But, for various reasons, the larger project was abandoned after a little more than a year. Nevertheless, I was still able to interview and document the work of my favorite Colorado *santera,* Teresa May Duran, questioning her about her personal history and training, as well as her methods and subjects, before discontinuing the larger project.[1]

I had met Duran in December of 2012 at the Winter Session of the Spanish Market while on a trip to Santa Fe, New Mexico, with my then wife, Jennifer. We had talked our way into an exclusive "members only" evening with the artists and their work, and were quickly drawn to a booth occupied by a lovely woman with dark, gentle eyes, and her devoted husband, who was happily assisting her. Although there were many fabulous artists there whose work we admired, such as Peter Ortega,

Charlie Carillio, and Catherine Robles-Shaw (another important Colorado-based *santera),* we fell in love with Teresa Duran, both for her gentle humility and her unique style and symbolism.

Looking at Duran's work, I immediately noted small details and unusual innovations in her depictions of traditional Spanish Colonial subjects, as well as highly traditional approaches to non-traditional subjects, that caught my interest. The details and innovations spoke of a personal devotion influencing her work that set it apart from the many other highly skilled artists at the market who sometimes focused more on technique and artistry than the devotional use for which the objects were originally intended. It was clear that Duran was both an artist and a devotee, which was the *santero* ideal in which I was most interested. I then remembered that I had read about her in a little booklet profiling several Colorado *santeros* who had participated in an exhibit at Regis University in Denver, Colorado in the late 1990s. We struck-up a conversation and she soon confirmed my intuitions about the personal details and symbolism in her work.

After purchasing a few smaller works from her, we exchanged information, and the next week I drove down to Arvada. Colorado, from my home in Boulder with a photographer to interview her and document her work and techniques.[2] Duran graciously invited us into her home and spoke openly of her life, her influences, and her own techniques, honed over more than two decades of experimentation. The interviews were illuminating, and Duran was exactly what I was hoping to find, a genuine 'saint-making' devotee in the modern world.

In this small monograph, I have completed a simple ethnographic study of Teresa Duran as a Colorado-based *santera,* detailing her life, the origins of her interest in the Spanish Colonial arts, her training as a *retablo*-maker, her craft (including her materials, methods of preparation, and techniques of application), as well as her style, choice of subjects, and ideals. As such, I hope it will be a small contribution to the understanding and appreciation of the traditional arts of Colorado from the Spanish Colonial period.

— Netanel Miles-Yépez
Crestone, Colorado, August 17th, 2018

The Making of a Colorado Santera

TERESA MAY DURAN is a respected Colorado *santera* who, like many latter-day practitioners of the art, took up 'saint-making' only later in life while raising a family and pursuing another career. However, in her case, the seeds of what would become an obsession with this New Mexican and Coloradan art form seem to have been planted early.

Born in Pueblo, Colorado in 1955, her father, Henry Martinez King, was a barber and part-time rancher, while her mother, Eva Barela Maldonado, raised Teresa and her siblings at home. Both parents were from Huerfano County in Southern Colorado, her father being born and raised in Red Wing, and her mother in La Veta, in the foothills of the Spanish Peaks.

Teresa's great-great grandfather, José Victorio Maldonado, who was born in Taos, homesteaded at the base of the Spanish Peaks in the 1870s. In time, the ranch where he raised sheep and grazed cattle grew to over 1,000 acres. This was considered a family tradition, as the Maldonados were originally shepherds from the Basque region of Spain.

Teresa's mother, Eva, came from a large family of 14 children, and only attended school up to the third grade, as she was needed at home to help her mother with chores and to take care of the younger children. Among her chief duties were making the tortillas and bread for the family. Indeed, she was so identified with this task that her brothers and sisters called her the *panadera,* the 'bread-maker.' According to Duran, "She was the most wonderful cook, and very creative. She was a great inspiration in my life."

Teresa's paternal great-grandfather was James King, an Anglo homesteader who came up the Santa Fe Trail in the 1860s. His son, Charles King, later married into a Hispanic ranching family in Huerfano County named Martinez, originally from the Taos area. Santana Martinez, his wife, was the granddaughter of Donaciana Manchego, origianlly from Abiquiú, who came into Colorado in the 1860s as well.

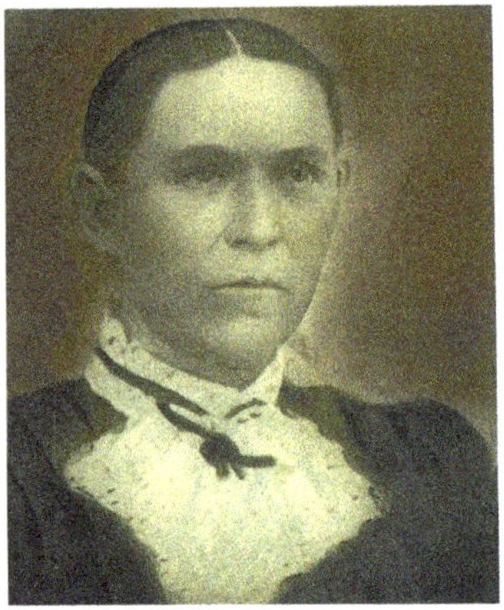

Donaciana Manchego Ames

In 1965, when Teresa was about ten years old, her father Henry bought a small ranch in Chama, Colorado, to which the family would retreat on weekends. Shortly after he had purchased the land, he took Teresa with him as he went to look over the property. About 300 feet from the house was an old, two-room adobe structure with a cross out front and a padlock on the door. Breaking the padlock, her father entered the dark structure with Teresa trailing just behind. It was a *morada*, a meeting-house of the Penitente Brotherhood, a Hispanic fraternity of Catholic laymen who functioned as pious guardians for the communities of Southern Colorado and New Mexico.[3]

Entering the starkly contrasting light and shadow of the *morada*, Teresa describes her experience that day and what she saw next:

> We walk in and we see the first room, which was like a storage room, where they kept the things they used in their ceremonies. That's where all the noise-makers *[matracas]* and the flagellation whips *[disciplinas]* were kept. I remember they had a wooden candle-holder *[tenebrario]* with candles all in a pyramid-like form. Both the wooden noise-makers and the candle-holder were huge!
>
> Then we walk into the chapel. The altar was still intact, and there were *bultos* at each side of the altar. I remember there were also chests filled with clothes that they used to change out the clothing of the statues for different ceremonies. And there were *retablos* along all the walls, along with Stations of the Cross.
>
> Now, my dad was a very tall man, about six foot, and he wore cowboy boots and a hat all the time. And here I was this little girl, you know, ten years old. Well, we walked into that

> room, on those old warped wood floors, and his cowboy boots and his being a big man caused the floor to shake; and all of a sudden, the hands on the saints started to move! 'Cause, you know, the old *bultos* were not fully wood. The body of it is like a cloth doll, and they attached the carved hands and head to that so they could dress it like a doll. So when my dad's weight shook the floors, the hands started to sway, and my father, right away, starts making the sign of the cross, and I'm looking around with my eyes wide, like, *'What's going on in here!'*"

After this experience, Teresa's father would tease her, "Don't go by the *morada* at night!" But it was too late; she was magnetically drawn to the building and its objects. For the next three or four years, she would go and explore the *morada* on her own, looking at its *retablos* and *bultos*, picking up the big *matracas* and swinging them until they made their distinctive sound.[4] But, after a time, her father began to worry over the burden of being the guardian of these sacred objects, no longer in use and soon to be extremely valuable. So, around 1969, he sought out one of the last *penitentes* left in the area, a man in his 80s named Valdez, and asked him if he would come and remove the belongings of the Penitente Brotherhood.[5]

About six months after the artifacts had been removed, Teresa remembers how a little twister came down from the mountains and hit the *morada*, destroying the roof and throwing all the *vigas* (beams) off the top of the adobe structure. The twister landed right on what has now been identified as the historic Las Crestones Morada, and strangely enough, touched nothing else in the area. Teresa commented on how a neighbor, Abe Bravo, had a large pile of loose hay just fifty yards away from the structure that was completely undisturbed. Without the roof and the *vigas,* the old adobe building was quickly worn down by the elements until only the foundation remained.[6] Teresa's brothers, Wayne and Henry Jr., still own the ranch.

As a child growing up in Pueblo, Colorado, Teresa described herself as a mediocre and indifferent student who, nevertheless, always loved to draw and make things. "I used to get into trouble by drawing on things," she remembers. "One time, I made all these little puppets out of my dad's black electrical tape—He was really angry! Another time, while my mother was sewing, I took a pair of her scissors and pulled up the fabric of my dress into little peaks and cut the tops off to make patterns. By the time my mother looked at me, I had holes all over my dress! So I think I was

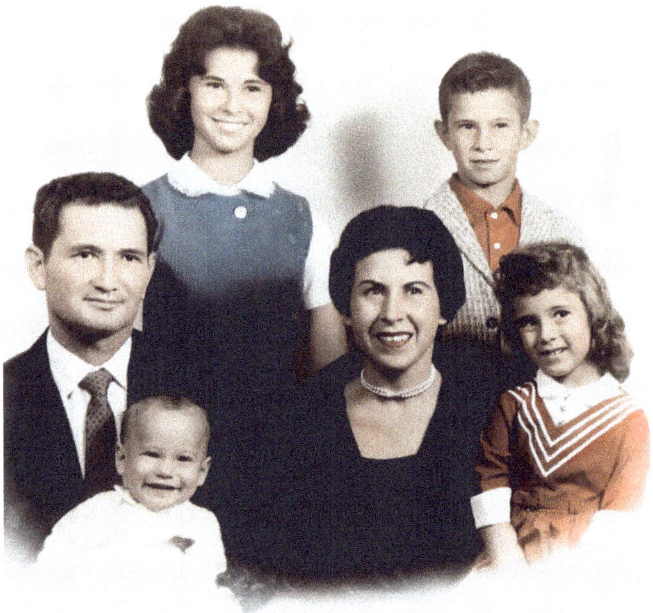

The King-Maldonado family. Teresa King at the bottom right.

fascinated with shapes and colors since I was really young."

After graduating from Pueblo's South High School in 1973, Teresa went to live with an aunt Sara in Santa Ana, California for a year, where she worked in a factory, soldering diodes on computer boards. Unsatisfied with this work, she returned to Colorado to go to college. In high school, she had been in a program called Upward Bound, which targeted students from low-income and minority families for special attention in order to prepare them for college. With the confidence she had gained in this program, she applied and was accepted to the University of Southern Colorado in Pueblo, where she studied social work. But, even then, she could not wholly abandon her love of art and enthusiastically took a class on the art of the Southwest. As a part of the class, the students took a special field trip to Santa Fe, New Mexico, to see the traditional *retablos* and *bultos* in the museums there.

When she had completed her Associate Degree in human service work, Teresa was undecided about her next steps. She began to take classes toward a Bachelor's Degree, but wasn't completely certain of her aim. So she went to live with her sister, Caroll, in Santa Fe for a time to consider her options. Not long after, while visiting her parents in Pueblo at the Christmas holiday, she ran into a young man she had once dated. His name was Ernest Duran Jr. and he was studying law at the University of Colorado at Boulder. Happy to have reunited, but doubtful about long-distance relationships, he asked her if she would come to Boulder. To his surprise, she said, "Yes," and the two were married shortly after.

After finishing Law School, Ernest got an internship with the National Labor Relations Board in Houston, Texas, where the couple lived for a short time. He was then offered a job with the same in Denver, where he afterward had a long career in labor relations and the couple raised their three children—Ernest III, Crisanta, and Caroll.

When her youngest child was about three years old, Teresa decided to finish her Bachelor's Degree at Metropolitan State College of Denver. The stress of social work no longer seemed manageable while raising her children, so she pursued a new degree in business administration. She later got a job working for the City of Arvada in affordable housing, and after two years, went to work for the State of Colorado, developing affordable housing all over Colorado. Eventually, she worked her way up to Deputy Director. While filling-in as Interim Director over a six-month period in 2009, she was offered the position of Director. But, at that point, Teresa decided, "Time is short," and retired so that she could dedicate herself to painting *santos* full-time.

Over the years, she had painted whenever she could find the time, mostly as a hobby. But sometime in the early 1990's, Teresa bumped into an old friend from the University of Southern Colorado—Meggan Rodríguez DeAnza—while attending a Chicano art show at the Denver Art Museum. Although they had lost touch many years before, they recognized one another immediately. In the interim, Meggan had gotten her Master's Degree in Art and had pursued a career as an art teacher in the Denver school system. As both shared a love of painting, the two began to rekindle their friendship. At the time, Teresa was mostly painting watercolors and showed them to Meggan, who suggested that she might be good at painting *retablos*. She then showed her some that she had painted herself while living in Taos, New Mexico, and Teresa fell in love with them.

Encouraged and inspired by Meggan's work, Teresa slowly started to imitate and produce her own renderings of traditional *santos* in acrylic paint on pre-cut wood from the store. Then, in the early 1990s, she participated in an art show at the Denver Botanical Gardens for the Chile Harvest Festival. There she met a *retablo* painter and colleague named Juan Martinez who told her that she could easily work with the traditional materials, using the traditional techniques. He said, "Teresa, this is what you do" and began to tell her how to make the gesso, giving her "around-about" measurements. Teresa remembers, "I wrote it down—and being the daughter of a fabulous cook that could throw anything together—he told me things, and I picked it up very quickly. I mean I just went to the stove and I did the animal skin glue like he told me, put the gesso together, and it just came out!" But she did not make the transition to natural pigments as quickly. She first began to paint in watercolor on the homemade gesso, and then tried a combination of watercolor and natural pigments before becoming comfortable enough to use the latter exclusively.

Once she found that she could actually do it all herself, Teresa became passionate about the traditions and the entire process of saint-making. She began to buy the available books on *santos* and the work of *santeros*, and to ask questions of whomever was willing to teach her a thing or two. In this way, she learned where should could obtain cochineal, how to cook-down chamisa, and how to use alum to make her colors more vibrant. She also started to study Christian symbolism and sacred art in her spare time, especially Byzantine and Spanish Colonial art (the influence of which are both still visible in her work). On vacations in the American Southwest and South America, she and her husband made a point of visiting places that had examples of Spanish Colonial art as it developed in these regions; and in each of them, Teresa found new inspiration which she brought into her painting. Indeed, her passion for her new craft and the use of natural materials even started to creep into her professional life. Working for the state, Teresa often had to travel around Colorado inspecting housing and meeting with other public officials. And often, in the course of a car ride through the mountains, colleagues would not be surprised to hear her cry out suddenly, *"Stop the car! Look at that dirt!* We gotta' pick up some of that dirt!" Then they would watch in amusement as she got out of the car to collect a little red or black dirt in a cup or bag to take home and use as a pigment.

Through the years, Teresa's painting has become more refined as she has achieved greater mastery over the medium. Nevertheless, her distinct style and bold presentation of evocative imagery has remained a constant from the beginning. Her work is distinguished from that of many others by her attention to symbolic detail and cultural context, by the incorporation of stylistic elements from both Spanish Colonial art of different regions and Byzantine iconography, and by her excellent color work. In each piece, there is a strong sense of story and the artist's commitment to depicting an important spiritual or moral ideal.

Although she received early recognition as a *santera*—her work being used on the posters for the Denver Chile Harvest Festival in 1995 and the "Santos: Sacred Art of Colorado" exhibit at the

O'Sullivan Arts Center of Regis University in 1997—Teresa found it difficult to find enough time for her passion until she finally retired in 2009. By then, she had already been a *santera* for 18 years and had participated in many shows and festivals in Colorado and New Mexico. Nevertheless, she had never applied to the famous Spanish Market in Santa Fe, New Mexico. It was something she felt she simply could not manage while working for the state. But as soon as she retired, she set to work on the difficult application process for the 2010 Market, and to her great surprise, was accepted on her first attempt. Since that time, Teresa has participated in both the Summer and Winter Spanish Markets every year, and continues to participate in exhibits and shows throughout Colorado and the greater Southwest, including the annual Rendezvous & Spanish Colonial Market of the Tesoro Cultural Center in Morrison, Colorado.

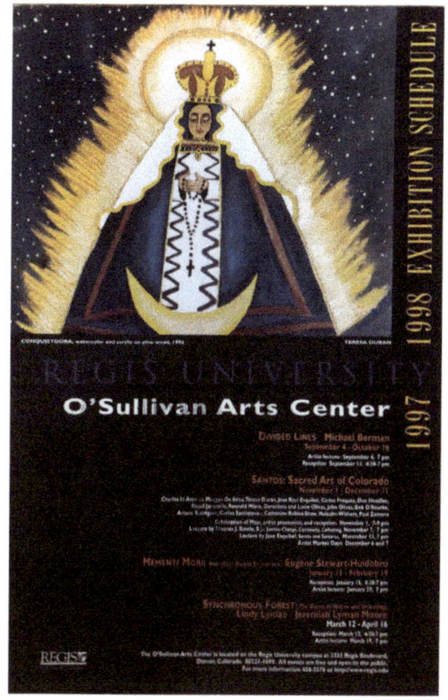

Today, Teresa and her husband divide their time between their home in Arvada, Colorado, and their ranch in Las Animas County, from which they can view the Spanish Peaks. When they are not traveling to a show, they like to visit different countries where Teresa can find new inspiration. Most recently, they visited Israel to soak up influences from the land of the Bible and the birthplace of Christianity.

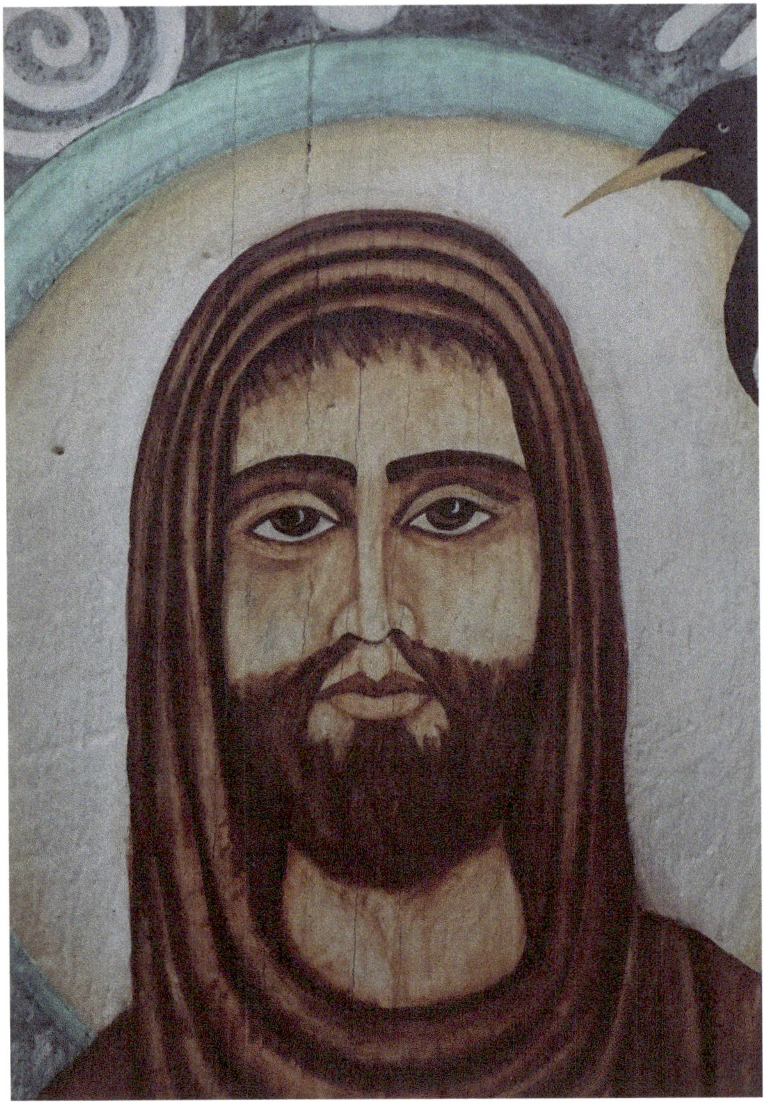

Detail of "Saint Francis, a Wild Soul." Natural pigments on wood.
(Photo by Amitai Zachary Malone, 2013)

The Art of a Colorado Santera

Unlike the period in which *retablos* were first produced in the New Mexico Territory as supports for personal worship on home altars and objects of veneration for churches and *moradas*, many are now sold to art collectors who purchase these works based on such secular considerations as artistic merit, relative market value, novelty and scarcity. Duran says she has often heard collectors at the Spanish Market taking excitedly about "a new artist," and of how they "need to collect their work early before the prices go up," but is herself most pleased when a *retablo* is sold to someone who is moved by it spiritually:

> I think it's wonderful if a church buys your work;[7] but for me, it's for the person who is moved by it, or who believes that this saint could be an intermediary for what they are praying about. . . . I think when a person buys the work from me, and I know it's moved them spiritually, that's the satisfaction for me.

For this reason, Duran most often chooses subjects by which she is herself moved, or to which she believes others may feel connected. On the back of each *retablo*, she gives the name of the saint, sometimes with a short handwritten description. On the back of a particular San Francisco (St. Francis) in her workshop was written, "Patron Saint of Dysfunctional Families and the Environment." While many *santeros* will call St. Francis "Patron Saint of Animals," or "of Nature," Duran chooses to draw attention to the fact that the saint had a difficult relationship with his father, thus making him accessible in new ways to potential buyers who might wish his intercession with this all too common problem.

Between 2010 and 2012, Duran made numerous *retablos* of recurring subjects, such as: Nuestra Señora de Guadalupe (Our Lady of Guadalupe), San Francisco de Asís (Saint Francis of Assisi), La Conquistadora (The Conqueress), Nuestra Señora de los Dolores (Our Lady of Sorrows), San Pascual Bailon (Saint Paschal Baylon), La Santa Trinidad (The Holy Trinity), and San Isidro Labrador (Saint Isadore the Laborer). Many of these *retablos* were given descriptive titles reflecting their unique content, such as: "Our Lady of Guadalupe with Large Moon," "Our Lady of Guadalupe with Milagros," "Saint Francis with Bird Halo," "Saint Francis Above the Trees," "Saint Francis with Magpie," "Saint Francis, a Wild Soul," "Stigmatas of Saint Francis," "San Ysidro Harvesting Melons, and "Saint Isadore with Corn and Chickens."

In the same period, Duran also made *retablos* of non-traditional or rarely recurring subjects, such as: "Our Lady of Conquering Love," "San Librada," "Santa Teresa," "Santa Rita," "San Patricio," "Santa Lucia," "Saint Theresa the Little Flower," "Saint Michael and the Lost Souls," "Sacred Heart of Jesus," "Our Lady of Oaxaca," "Saint Michael," "Padre Pio," "Madonna and Child," "The Holy Family," "Saint Vincent of Zaragoza, Patron of Wine and Vineyards," "Santa Cecilia as a Mariachi, Patroness of Music," "Our Lord of Sorrows, Patron of Workers," "San Raphael, Patron Saint for Healing," "Saint Anne reading to the Virgin Mary, Patroness of Grandchildren," "Saint Gertrude, Patroness of Cats," "Saint Joseph with the Child Jesus, Patron of a Peaceful Death, Workers, and Families," "La Purísima of the Apocalypse," and "Modern Archangels" (with San Miguel holding a lasso to rope Satan, San Rafael holding a fishing pole, and San Gabriel with an iPhone, as patron of communication—all of them wearing cowboy boots).

"La Conquistadora" Retablos

A notable example of creative variability in depicting the same basic image can be seen in a series of Duran's Conquistadoras. La Conquistadora is perhaps the most cherished image of the Virgin Mary in all of the original New Mexico Territory, and is a favorite subject of many modern *santeros* in New Mexico and Colorado, including Duran.

In 1996, Duran was one of ten *santeros* commissioned to contribute to a special *reredos* (altarscreen) that was to be installed in the permanent Regis Collection of *santos* in the

Dayton Memorial Library at Regis University in Denver, Colorado. For this *reredos,* she painted a La Conquistadora in watercolor and acrylic on pine wood. At this point, she had obviously not yet made the transition to the exclusive use of natural pigments, but was already displaying elements of what would become her signature style—bold color and imagery with the use of personally significant natural backgrounds. In this case, La Conquistadora is dressed in the navy blue of the night sky, closely matching her star-studded background, and is lit from behind her head by a bright yellow aureole, making her appear like the "woman clothed with the sun," spoken of in Revelation 12:1. Even the moon at her feet is yellow like the aureole, suggesting that this Madonna is herself the brightest star in the heavens for us, and the sun of our solar system.

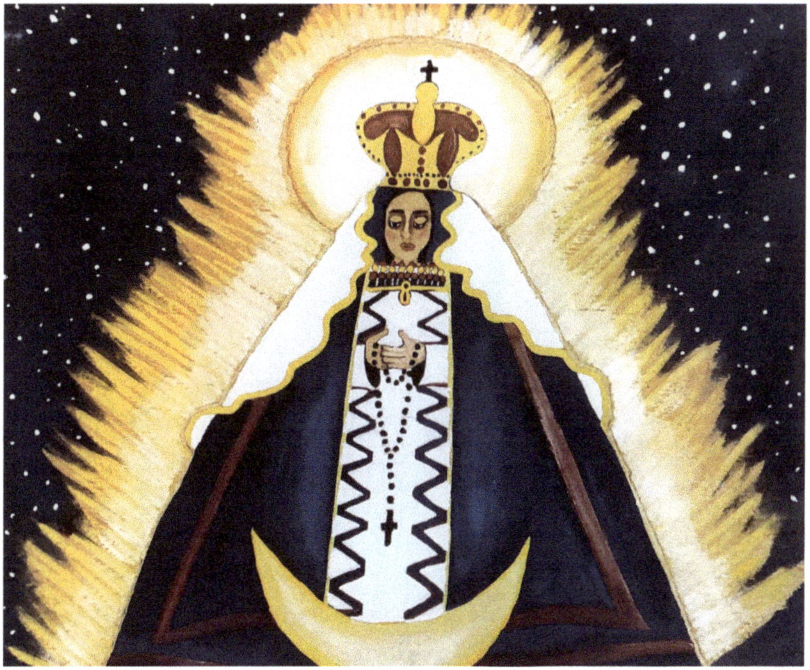

"Conquistadora." Watercolor and acrylic on pine. 1996. Collection Regis University.

In a series of Conquistadoras painted more than a decade later, we can see a definite maturation in her style, as well as her sense of design, color and composition. Among the most interesting of these is her "La Conquistadora with Holy Spirit" painted in 2012, which not only shows the influence of Peruvian color schemes and design on her work, but the personally significant addition of a descending dove, symbolic of the Holy Spirit in Christian art. This symbol—which has its origins in the verse from the Gospels (John 1:32), "I saw the Spirit descending from Heaven like a dove, and it remained on him"—was added to the Conquistadora image as testimony of a very personal experience while visiting the actual shrine of

La Conquistadora statue in the Cathedral Basilica of St. Francis of Assisi in Santa Fe, New Mexico:

> In the last years of my mother's life, she lived in Santa Fe. And I would go to Santa Fe for three or four days, once a month, to visit her. And one of the things we used to do is go to the chapel where La Conquistadora statue is. I would take her in, help her get out of the wheelchair, and she would kneel at the altar and pray. One day, I did the same routine—because we always did this—and took her up, knelt her down, lit some candles, and I went back to sit in the pews. I wasn't really even thinking of anything in particular. I was just sitting there and glanced over at my mother, when all of a sudden, I had this feeling of something coming and entering in my body. It was something I could not control, a kind of ecstatic state, and it stayed within me probably for a good minute or two, and then it was gone. And I felt at that time that the Holy Spirit had entered my body.

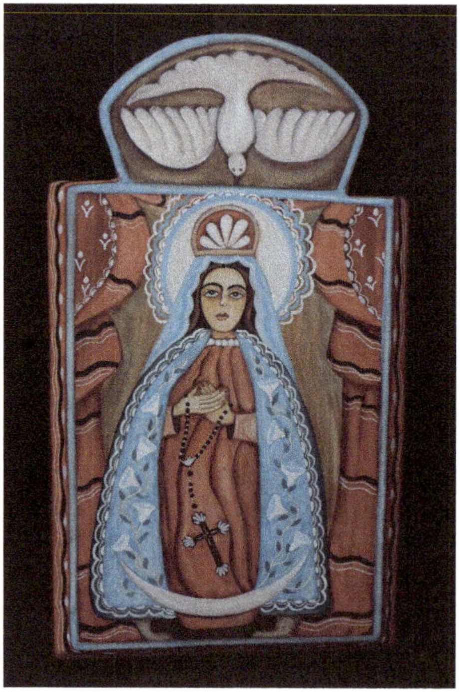

"La Conquistadora with the Holy Spirit." 2012.
(Photo by Amitai Zachary Malone, 2013)

This *retablo* also depicts La Conquistadora with a rosary instead of the Christ child, perhaps reflecting the devotion of Duran's mother at that time of this experience, and shows the lunar crescent at the Madonna's feet, more often associated with the Virgin of Guadalupe. The addition of the lunar crescent may also have affected the choice of blues and whites on the mantle, which suggest moonlight. The mantle itself is decorated with calla lilies, and the crown of La Conquistadora is made out of an outlined rosette, a traditional feature of New Mexican and Coloradan *retablos.*

Another *retablo* in this series, "La Conquistadora Over Santa Fe" painted in 2010, is less informed by personal experience, but better contextualizes La Conquistadora in the natural environment and associates her with the Cathedral Basilica of St. Francis of Assisi. Duran also creates an association between the distinctive conical shape of La Conquistadora and the hills and mountains surrounding Santa Fe by placing her among them, as if she were their highest peak. More than a mere artistic association, Duran purposefully located the Madonna in the hills to suggest a direct relationship.

On a visit to Cusco, Peru, some years before, while looking at Spanish Colonial art, Duran noticed that many of their Madonnas were shaped like hilltops. Intrigued by this phenomenon, she did her own research and found that the Incas had considered the mountains sacred and worshipped at them, and that this part of their culture had been absorbed into the Catholicism of the region and showed itself in the unusual shape of their Madonnas.

Remembering this, Duran wished to say something in "La Conquistadora Over Santa Fe" about the indigenous elements that come into Spanish Colonial art, as well as something about the unique genetic and cultural fusion of the Hispanic peoples of North and South America. This message can also be seen in the Native American shawl spread across the Madonna's shoulders.

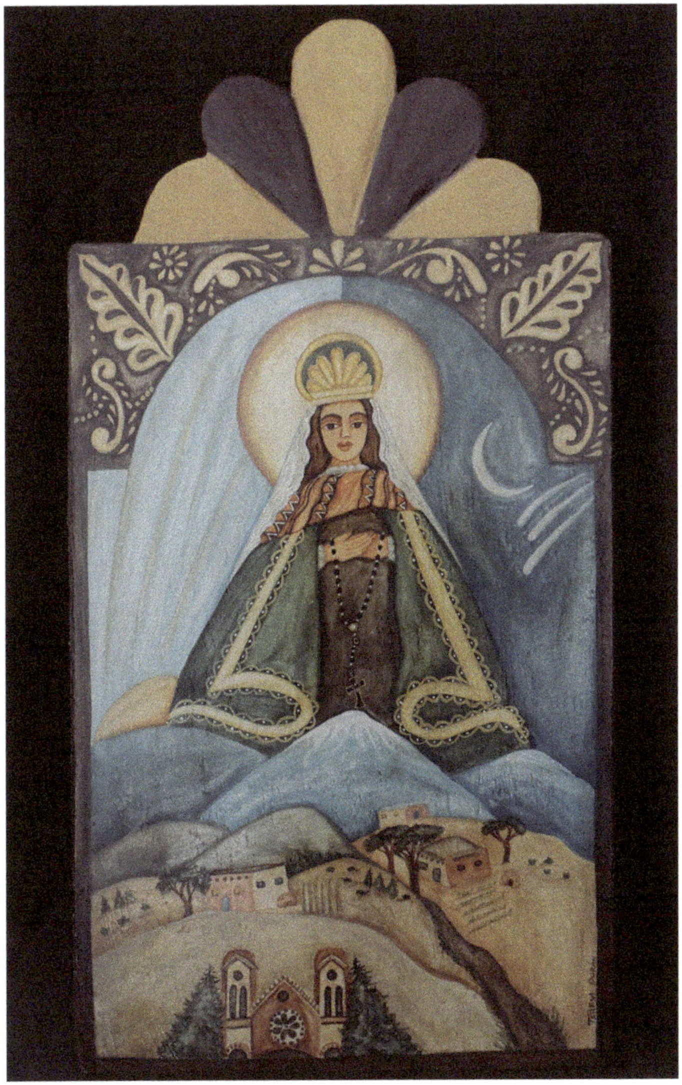

"La Conquistadora over Santa Fe." 2010.
(Photo by Amitai Zachary Malone, 2013)

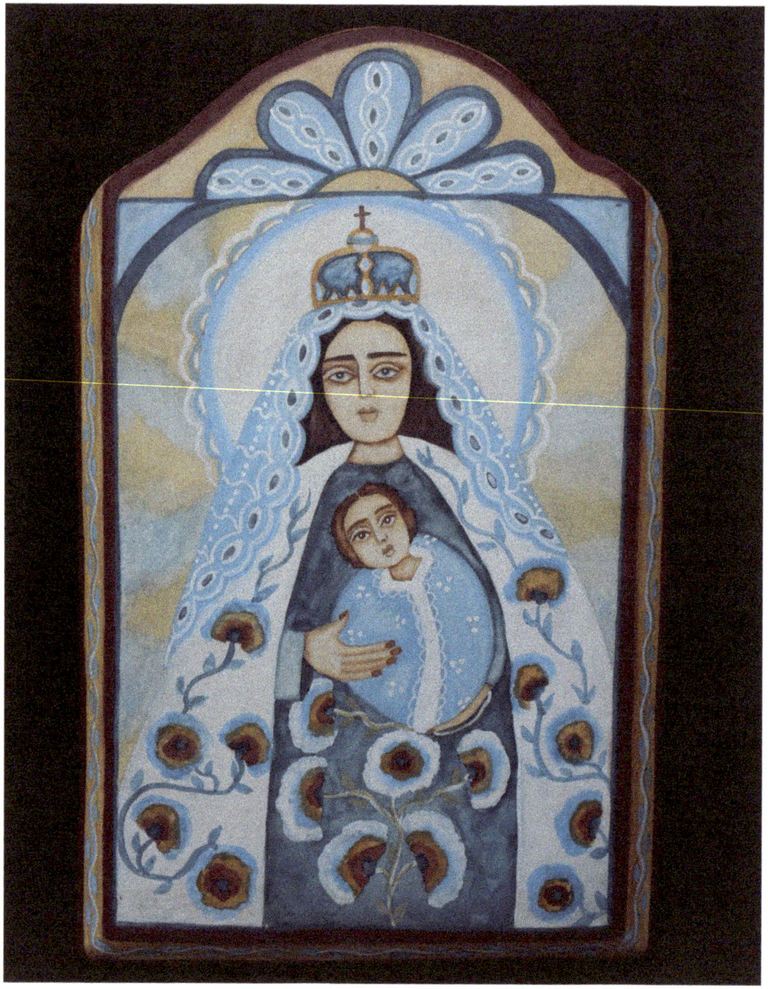

"La Conquistadora with Colcha Dress." 2012.
(Photo by Amitai Zachary Malone, 2013)

In this *retablo*, we again see the rosary depicted in place of the Christ child, suggesting a devotional relationship to the Madonna, and the rosette crown. In the background is a divided sky, depicting sunset and full night. The sunset shows the sun descending behind the hills, its rays still streaking the sky, while the night scene shows a crescent moon accompanied by shooting stars (a personally significant theme seen in many of Duran's *retablos*).

A last *retablo,* "La Conquistadora with Colcha Dress" painted in 2012, also reflects local associations; in this case, the actual 'wardrobe' of the Conquistadora installed on the shrine in the Cathedral Basilica of St. Francis of Assisi in Santa Fe. Like many such Madonnas, La Conquistadora has different specially made gowns for different occasions. This *retablo* depicts a particular gown with special *colcha* embroidery made for La Conquistadora by a local *colchera* and Santa Fe native, Julia R. Gómez. Seeing this particularly beautiful gown, made with one of the unique arts of the region, Duran felt compelled to make a *retablo* of La Conquistadora (this time with Christ child and a more traditional crown) wearing the gown actually made for her by *colchera*, Julia Gómez.

La Purísima of the Apocalypse

Unlike many *santeros*, Duran is comfortable with, and genuinely inspired to paint *retablos* of less conventional subjects. A good example is her "La Purísima of the Apocalypse," or Our Lady of the Apocalypse (ca. 2012). One day, while her husband was reading the New Testament, he drew her attention to Revelation 12:1-3, describing a vision of a "woman clothed with the sun, with the moon under her feet, and a crown of twelve stars on her head" and a "great red dragon, having seven heads." Inspired by the description, she began to conceive of her own interpretation of the image including wings on the Woman Clothed with the Sun and God the Father above.

Apart from its unusual subject matter, it is also a particularly successful piece with other interesting features and innovations. Instead of merely fitting the subject into the usual rectangular *retablo* format topped with a simple rosette, Duran chose and cut a long board to suit the subject matter, adding a frame of aged wood (from her husband's grandfather's old sawmill decorated with rusty *clavos* from Mexico) on top of the *retablo* to separate elements of the painting, such as God the Father at the top and the Great Red Dragon at the bottom. She had seen old wood used in this way on *retablos* from Mexico.

The face of La Purísima is interesting in that particles of marble dust on the surface of the gesso create an interesting effect, their texture catching the natural pigments in an unusual way. Such effects are a result of using traditional methods and materials.

Recurring Motifs and Unusual Subject Matter

In many of Duran's *retablos*, one notices a number of recurring themes and decorative background elements. For instance, depictions of San Francisco (Saint Francis) will often feature wolves and magpies. The wolf, of course, is commonly associated with the hagiographic accounts of the life of San Francisco, as are birds. But the magpie is a particular detail added by Duran because of her own appreciation of them and their prevalence in Colorado and New Mexico. Likewise, Duran's San

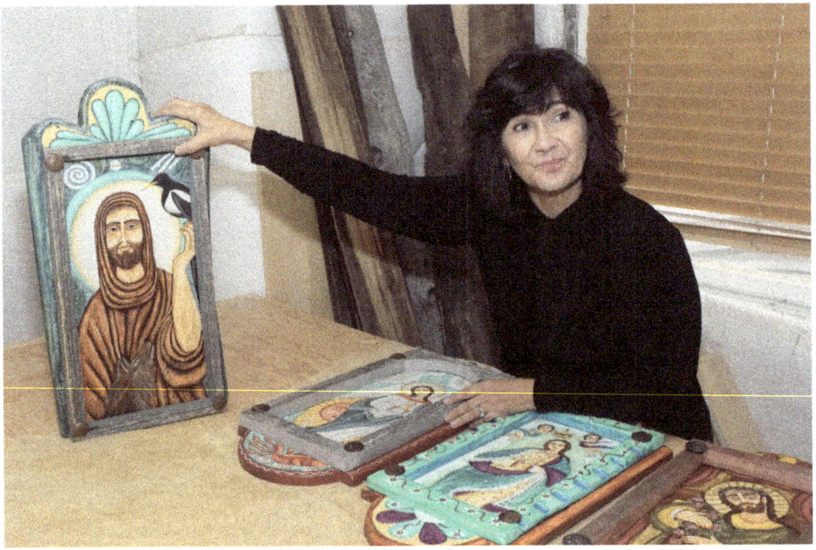

Duran displaying "San Francisco, a Wild Soul" (2012) *retablo* in her workshop.
(Photo by Amitai Zachary Malone, 2013)

Francisco *retablos* often have (because of his association with nature) "a wild background, with comets and the Milky Way." This feature she attributes to "dreams of comets shooting through the sky" she has had since childhood.

These personal elements reflect Duran's desire to experiment with both symbols and subject matter. In her opinion, the economic lure of reproducing the same image over and over can cause one to lose one's interest in the work, as well as one's creative edge. And though she does create many smaller, more affordable works of popular saints, she tries to make each *retablo* unique, and uniquely appealing to different potential buyers. But to challenge herself as an artist, she likes to depict less traditional images, often on larger boards.[8]

The Craft of a Colorado Santera

When asked why she would put in the effort of using the traditional methods and materials, Duran simply smiles and says, "you get into it, and then you just love it." Though she has mostly focused on perfecting her craft through the years, she has taught classes on *retablo* making for Tony Ortega, an artist in Denver and professor at Regis University. She has also taught the traditional methods of making gesso to a few personal friends over the years.

Traditional Materials

The first major consideration of traditional *santeros* concerns what materials they will use and where they will obtain them. As artisans preserving a traditional art-form, many *santeros* attempt to use locally sourced materials whenever possible or a close approximation of materials that would have been known to the earliest practitioners of the saint-making art in Colorado. For a *retablo* maker like Duran, this includes the type of wood on which she will paint her saints.[9]

Choosing and Carving the Wood Panels

Duran obtains most of the wood for her *retablos* from Robinson Sawmill in Weston, Colorado, located near her ranch in Las Animas County, and from Frank Paxton Lumber Company in Denver, Colorado. However, she is also offered wood by friends and family on occasion, and sometimes recovers wood from old structures or finds it in various other places.

When buying recently milled wood, Duran looks for lower density wood without knots that is easier to carve, such as Pine, Aspen, Basswood and Engelmann Spruce. Older, more rustic wood, she sometimes uses for framing, and occasionally for an actual *retablo*. Although this old wood is very dry and particularly hard to work with for *retablos*, having a tendency to splinter when cut or carved, Duran will sometimes choose to work with it because its size is more suitable for the image she wants to make, or because she wishes the rippling texture of the old wood to be part of the final image.

If the wood from the sawmill is not yet the right size for the piece, Duran has a table saw on which she can cut it down to the right dimensions. From there, she can sketch the outline of the *retablo*, including traditional features like a rosette at the top or other simple features which she cuts out with a band or scroll saw.

One interesting feature of older *retablos,* noted by Duran, is a slight rounding of the surface rising up from the long edges of the *retablo.* She suspects that the *santeros* of the past were using scrap wood leftover from the milling process. The flat boards would be too valuable for most *santeros* to purchase, being needed for construction, but the rounded scrap left over from the process, once the bark had been removed, made an inexpensive alternative. Thus, Duran sometimes tries to obtain such scrap leftover from the milling process, or occasionally rounds the edges of some pieces herself to give them the look of older *retablos.*

Once the board is cut into the desired shape, Duran can begin the carving process with a simple set of hand tools, wearing protective gloves and an apron. For her simple rosettes, the outside shape is made with the scroll saw, but the inner furrows on the surface are made by scoring over a pencil line with a crescent shaped knife blade, which might also be used for cutting away on either side of the scored line to create the furrow. The furrow, says Duran, must be made fairly deep so that it is not obscured by the layers of gesso which will be applied later. Duran keeps it simple and does not do a lot of carving on her *retablos*, focusing more on painting. But she does try to keep up the tradition of doing some carving, and occasionally cuts into the surface to create a slight relief effect.

On some larger pieces of wood, which she does not wish to make smaller by cutting away with a scroll saw, or for the rounded scrap wood from the milling process, Duran will cut special rosettes or other decorations to be attached to the main board. To do this, she will drill holes into the sides of both the main board and the attachments, then attach them with pins and glue, or screws.

Once the boards are carved and assembled, she fills-in any knots or holes with wood putty, allows it to dry and then sands the boards by hand in preparation for applying the gesso.

Making and Applying the Gesso

To make the marble dust gesso for her *retablos*, Duran first makes a mixture of animal skin glue (usually purchased from art supply stores catering to professional artists, or on-line suppliers of high-quality art supplies) and water. She measures out one cup of animal skin glue pellets to mix with nine cups of water. (When mixed with the marble dust, this makes enough gesso to cover a number of boards.) The animal skin glue and water are then mixed in a large glass bowl and stirred until the animal skin glue is completely dissolved. It is then put it in the refrigerator to set-up for approximately 12 hours. Duran often mixes the two in the evening and then leaves it in the refrigerator overnight. After 12 hours, the animal skin glue mixture should have the consistency of cold *menudo* or a Jell-O mold.

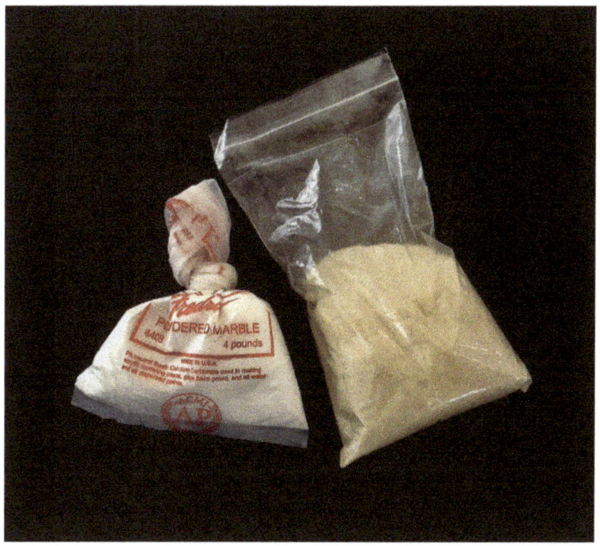

Duran's marble dust and animal skin glue.
(Photo by Netanel Miles-Yépez, 2018)

Before she begins to cook down the animal skin glue, Duran places newspapers on the floor and over her countertops as well as her kitchen and dining room tables. She then lays out all the boards that are ready to be gessoed. (If she is preparing for the Spanish Market, there may be as many as 30 boards.)

When these preparations are complete, Duran puts the gelatinous animal skin glue mixture in a large, heavy bottomed stainless steel pot. She then begins to heat the pot on a very low temperature, slowly stirring as the glue is liquefied. The heavy bottom and low temperature are necessary so as not to burn the glue.

When the glue is completely liquefied, Duran begins to add marble dust (purchased in three-pound bags from a local art supply store catering to professional artists) while continuing to stir. For this step she wears a mask so as not to inhale the dust. She adds the dust, as needed, and stirs until she gets the consistency desired, something she describes as being like a "thin pancake batter."

Then, keeping the heat very low, she takes out a flat, high-quality soft-bristle brush, about an inch wide, and begins to cover the top and sides of the boards. Lower quality brushes tend to lose their bristles in the gesso and often create unwanted texture. For larger boards, she sometimes uses a large metal spoon to scoop the warm gesso onto the board before brushing. The gesso begins to dry almost immediately, so one must be careful of leaving fingerprints while handling the boards.

The consistency of Duran's gesso is thick enough that she is often able to cover her boards with a single thick coat, rather than the three or four often thought necessary. Her thick gesso also later allows her to do scrifitto on the *retablo* without it going back into the wood. "You want to do your scrifitto so it shows the design and it's on the gesso," she says.

Once coated, Duran carefully takes the board over to a table or surface where it can dry undisturbed for a minimum of 12 hours.

The Natural Pigments and Painting with Them

For painting the surface of the gessoed board, Duran mostly purchases her pigments from professional art supply retailers, but also collects them from nature when she can, or from local sources.[10] "You can't always be grinding everything," she says. The pre-ground turquoise she points out, she mixes with gum arabic, a dab of clove oil and water. But she adds, you have to be careful, because even a little too much of an ingredient can turn the mixture to mud.

The colors she uses are mostly "colonial colors," colors well known in Spanish Colonial artwork.

She points out her alum, saying, "When the weavers do the rugs, which are all natural pigments, they use this to activate the colors … The weavers boil their ingredients and add the alum to activate the color in it," to make the colors brighter.

Duran's current supply of cochineal *(Dactylopius coccus),* the small insect which is ground to make reds, was given to her in Oaxaca, Mexico, by a weaver from whom she brought a rug that is now on her dining room table. The weaver, she tells me, had a huge vat of cochineal. Cochineal in the United States can be very expensive to purchase, often selling for up to $50.00 per ounce. Duran's current supply was bought several years back, four ounces for $23.75. As a demonstration, using the bottom of a bowl of a spoon, Duran smashes one dry cochineal insect on a white piece of paper. The result is a rusty red powder. She says, "If you mix a little pinch of alum with the cochineal, you get the purplish red that you see in my pieces a lot." She adds, "Now, one of the artists told me she boils hers, and then boils it down and you get a more vibrant red. Or you can add lemon in it. And I've added lemon in it to get a different hue with not boiling." But she said, "If you add some lemon in it, it really gets bright red." Duran has not done this yet, but plans to soon to see if she can achieve a more vibrant red.

Chamisa (*Chrysothamnus nauseosus)*, she points out, is hard to use. You have to boil it down, but even then the result is grainy and not spectacular. Duran does not like to use it, especially when she can use pre-ground mineral pigments to better effect.

Her indigo is from India and she grinds it herself in a small wooden *molcajete.*

Piñon Sap Varnish and the Beeswax Coating

The final step in the *retablo*-making process is the application of a special piñon sap varnish and a beeswax coating. The Colorado Pinyon or Piñon Pine *(Pinus edulis)* grows mostly in Colorado, New Mexico, Arizona, and Utah, for the most part between 5,200 and 7,900 feet.[11] In the Spring, Duran often heads south to Huerfano and Las Animas counties to collect piñon sap, and often spends as much as half a day doing so, getting enough to keep herself stocked for some time. She then allows it to age as long as possible. New sap is very clear and makes a very shiny varnish. She prefers the molasses tint it acquires as it ages, which creates a nice antiqued look on the surface of the *retablo.* If possible, she collects older pieces of sap off the trees.

After receiving basic instructions from Juan Martinez, Duran eventually learned to make the piñon sap varnish in her own ingenious way. Because the sap is often filled with bits of tree bark,

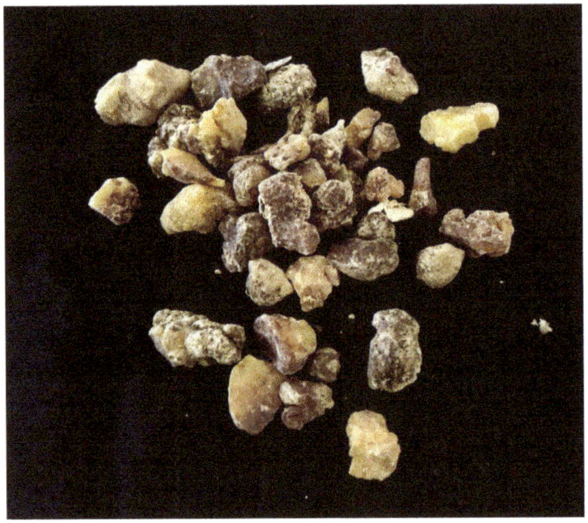

Dried piñon sap collected by Duran.
(Photo by Netanel Miles-Yépez, 2018)

pine needles and dirt, Duran puts the dry nuggets of piñon sap varnish in an old nylon sock and hangs it in a 16 oz. Mason jar. She fills the sock up, approximately 3 inches by 2 ½ inches with piñon nuggets, and then puts them on the bottom of the jar while the top of the sock hangs outside over the edge of the jar. The sock is left long enough to have at least half hanging outside of the jar. She then pours grain alcohol (Everclear) into the jar, filling it just enough to cover the piñon nuggets in the sock. She then covers it loosely and allows the piñon to dissolve in the alcohol for 24 hours, after which, she removes the sock full of bark, sticks and dirt, leaving a thin brown-tinted varnish ready for use.

If she finds that the varnish is too thick, she simply adds more alcohol. If it's too thin, the process has to be repeated. Duran seeks a consistency that spreads easily and dries within 24 hours (which is desirable when she is readying many pieces for a show). Also, she finds that thicker varnish also tends to be shinier and less desirable. It is a matter of taste, says Duran, noting that the straw appliqué artists prefer a very thick piñon sap varnish, as do some Colorado *santeros* like Frank Zamora, whose *retablos* are very shiny.

To spread the varnish, Duran uses a quality watercolor brush about an inch thick (as cheaper brushes tend to leave bristles in the varnish and do not create as smooth a surface).

When this is dry, Duran usually applies a light coat of beeswax with a lint free cloth to protect the varnish and reduce the sheen on it. After 20 minutes, she will then buff it with chamois or Elk hide. Duran uses natural beeswax (Toluene free) and always opens a window to get as much ventilation as possible when working with such products.

Afterword

Since 2013, Teresa Duran's style has continued to evolve, becoming more refined and richly colored. She continues to attend both the Colorado Spanish Market hosted by the Tesoro Cultural Center in Morrison, Colorado, and the Traditional Spanish Market of the Spanish Colonial Arts Society in Santa Fe, New Mexico, where there is frequently a waiting list for her artwork. Recently, Duran has accepted invitations to lecture on the traditonal arts of *retablo*-making at Regis University, and to teach classes on the art to artists and devotees.

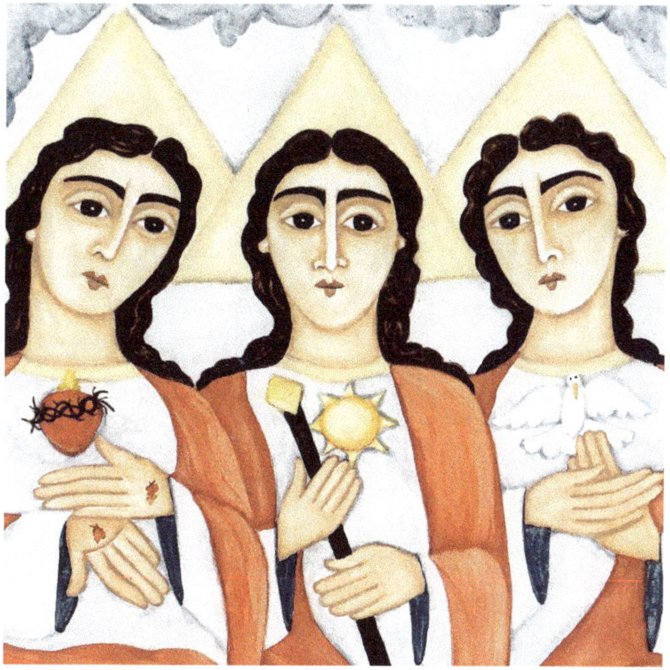

Detail from "La Santa Trinidad." 2018.
(Photo by Netanel Miles-Yépez, 2018)

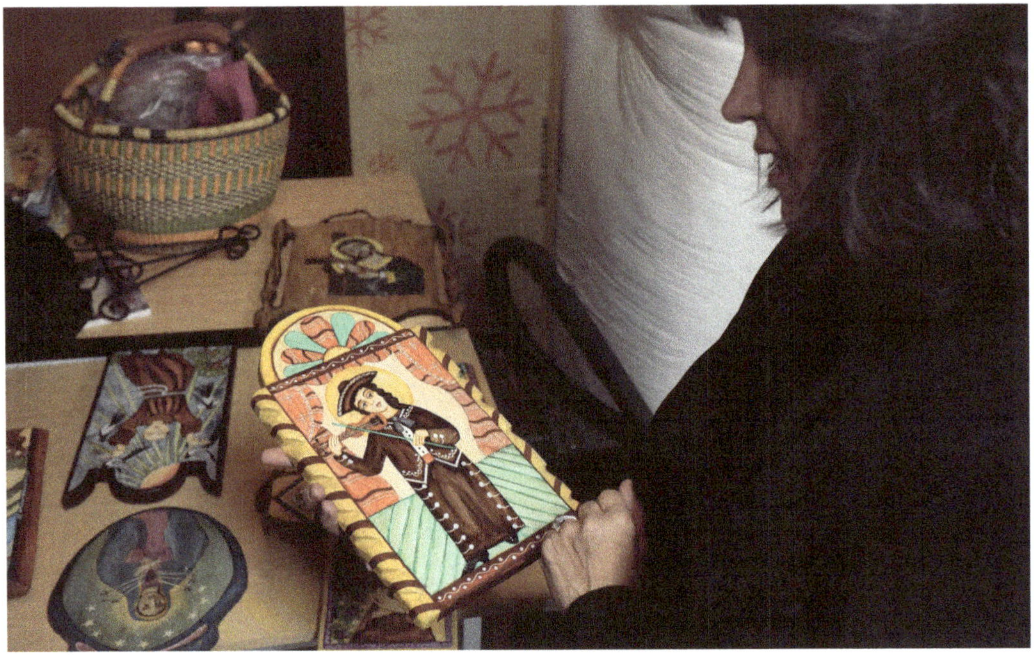

Duran holding her "Santa Cecilia as a Mariachi" (2012) *retablo* in her workshop.
(Photo by Amitai Zachary Malone, 2013)

Notes

1 The basic account of Duran's personal history and training, included herein, was originally published as an article, "The Making of Colorado Santera, Teresa May Duran," in *Delumin/a—Spirituality. Culture. Arts*. March 6th, 2014. (http://delumina.net/blog/2014/3/6/the-making-of-a-colorado-santera-teresa-may-duran)

2 I first interviewed Duran on December 14th, 2012, and again on February 22nd, 2013, following up with questions through e-mail correspondence on April 20th, 2013, and a last interview on August 25th, 2018 to verify details.

3 Of the Penitentes, Duran says: "I remember, when I was a little girl, my grandfather Maldonado, my mother's father, died when I was like five years old. And one of my earliest remembrances is going to his funeral. And the Penitentes came in and sang. Oh my goodness! The music and the way they used to sing . . . They'd wail; it was very scary for a little girl to hear that!"

4 Duran suspects that some of the work in the *morada* of her childhood may have been that of Francisco Vigil. 'I'm almost certain was the same style." The cross in the Church of Guadalupe, just down the road from her family property and the *morada* is credited to Francisco Vigil. She also thinks that the *morada* may be the Las Crestones Morada mentioned in a magazine article she had once read

5 Duran believes that some of those artifacts ended up in the collection of the Taylor Museum in Colorado Springs, "Because, later on, I did an art show with the Aurora Museum of History and they were able to borrow some of the Taylor Museum's things, and they had some of the *retablos* that I used to see as a little girl. And they were from Chama, Colorado."

6 Today, only a small portion of the foundation remains on the property now owned by Duran's brothers. The deed to this property shows that one acre was given to the Catholic Church where the *morada* stood. The prior owner was named Cardenas, which links it to the Los Crestones Morada.

7 Many churches might be inclined to buy larger works, such as a *reredos*. In her workshop, hung a *reredos* had made around 2008. It depicted St. Claire, St. Francis, St. Michael, God the Father, Jesus, and St. Rafael. At the top, the Holy Spirit says, *Viva Fuerte!* "Live strong!" I do not know if this was the only *reredos* she had made, or whether she had sold one prior to that date.

8 In the winter of 2013, Duran was painting a Tree of Life and planning a Noah's Ark. Duran's Tree of Life was adapted from a Greek Orthodox icon with depictions of the Twelve Apostles as fruit on the branches of the Tree, which she was replacing with symbols. Researching the Tree of Life in Christian contexts, she came upon St. Bonaventure's 13th century a description of the Tree of Life related to the stages of Jesus' life. To the original board, which then had only a sketch upon it, she intended to add *rosettas* (rosettes) attached with pins and a thin wood frame on top of the large *retablo.* Drilling holes, she would tap in fine nails, so as not to crack the rigid gesso.

9 In 2013, Duran was also considering taking up the tradition of painting on Elk hide, a tradition which very few Spanish Colonial artists have continued. She actually had a large Elk hide and explained that one does not paint on the smooth side, as one would expect, but on the soft side. The smooth side apparently does not absorb the paint as well, and much depends creating the right consistency with the paint. I do not know if she has since carried out an experiment with this art.

10 At the time, Duran was purchasing most of her pigments from earthpigments.com.

11 Duran had experimented with the sap of other trees, but found that they did not work as well.

Glossary

bulto (pl., bultos) – Wood-carved sculptures of saints, sometimes clothed like a doll.

colcha – Traditional rough embroidery of the New Mexico Territory.

colchera (masc., colchero) – Practitioner of the traditional rough embroidery.

disciplina (pl., disciplinas) – Flagellation whips used by the Penitente Brotherhood.

matraca (pl., matracas) – Wooden noise-makers used in the rituals of the Penitente Brotherhood.

morada (sing., moradas) – A meeting-house of the Penitente Brotherhood.

penitentes (sing., penitente) – A Hispanic fraternity of Catholic laymen who functioned as pious guardians for the communities of Southern Colorado and New Mexico.

reredos – Traditional altar screens painted by *santeros* for use in the meeting-houses of the Penitente Brotherhood.

retablo (pl., retablos) – Panted devotional panels.

santero (fem., santera) – A traditional saint-maker.

santo (pl., santos) – Saint.

tenebrario – a triangular wooden candle-holder.

Biographies

Netanel Miles-Yépez is an artist and religion scholar. His books include, *My Love Stands Behind a Wall: A Translation of the Song of Songs and Other Poems*, *A Heart Afire: Stories and Teachings of the Early Hasidic Masters,* and *The Common Heart: An Experience of Interreligious Dialogue*. As an artist, he is known for his vibrant and challenging oil paintings influenced by traditional religious imagery, set in a modern multicultural context. Currently he is a professor in the Department of Religious Studies at Naropa University, and divides his time between Boulder and Crestone, Colorado.

Teresa May Duran is a fifth generation Coloradoan, whose family can be traced to the early settlements of New Mexico. Her work as a *santera* has shown in various museums, universities, churches and galleries. Her artwork was selected to market the 1994 and 2011 "Chili Harvest Festival" in Denver, Colorado, and the 1997 and 2014, "Colorado Santeros" exhibit at Regis University. She has also won several awards for her *retablos* through the Tesoro Cultural Center. In 2010, Teresa was juried into the Spanish Market in Santa Fe, New Mexico. Her artwork may be seen at teresamayduran.com.

www.ingramcontent.com/pod-product-compliance
Ingram Content Group UK Ltd.
Pitfield, Milton Keynes, MK11 3LW, UK
UKHW060121010826
14089UKWH00006B/88

9 781953 22002